About this book

In Queen Victoria's time, Sunday was a day of rest and a holiday for everyone. The pictures in this book will show you how men and women and boys and girls spent their Sundays in England a hundred years ago. You can learn a great deal about the Victorians and their daily lives—the clothes they wore, the houses they lived in and the things they liked to do in their spare time.

In the morning, almost everyone went to church—father, mother, children and servants. In the afternoon, a family had a choice of many activities. Some families visited museums or art galleries, or walked in the parks. In the country they cycled or picnicked, or went to the seaside on the new excursion trains. Staying at home was popular, too. Father might read aloud, or the family would play games, watch a magic lantern show or have a musical evening. Look carefully at these pictures—they will tell you many things about life in England a hundred years ago.

Some of the words printed in *italics* may be new to you. You can look them up in the word list on page 92.

AN EYEWITNESS BOOK

A Victorian Sunday

JILL HUGHES

WAYLAND PUBLISHERS

More Eyewitness Books

Frontispiece: Victorian families enjoying the seaside at Ramsgate

SBN 85340 177 2
Copyright © 1972 by
Wayland Publishers Ltd
49 Lansdowne Place, Hove, East Sussex
2nd Impression 1976
Filmset by Keyspools Ltd, Golborne, Lancashire
Reproduced and printed by photolithography and bound in
Great Britain at The Pitman Press, Bath

Contents

Sunday Morning

Queen Victoria reigned from 1837 to 1901, and this period of history is called the *Victorian* Age. It has also been called "the Age of Faith" because Victorian men and women were deeply religious. Sunday was a "holy day" as well as a holiday for the Victorians. All *respectable* people began their Sunday mornings with family prayers and then went to church.

Most of the Victorians in this book belonged to what we should call the middle class. Some of them were quite well off—businessmen, lawyers or doctors. They were called professional men. Some were less well off—shopkeepers, poorer clergymen, clerks. But they were all comfortable. Even an office clerk could afford to employ a servant girl.

The Victorians believed in hard work and upright behaviour. They liked to look dignified. Their clothes covered them from chin to toe and were made of good, thick materials. Victorian houses were tall and thin and were often built of red brick. The kitchen and *scullery* were in the basement. The best parlour and the dining room were on the ground floor. The second and third stories contained the bedrooms. Bathrooms were very rare and so was plumbing of any kind. Each bedroom had a jug and a basin for washing. The servants had their little rooms in the attic.

THE BASEMENT KITCHEN. A maid servant was always the first person to get up on Sunday morning. Her first job was to light the fire in the kitchen stove. Then she boiled water and took it upstairs for the family to wash. Her mistress only came into the kitchen to give instructions about the day's meals— she never did any kitchen work herself.

BUYING MILK. The servant could buy fresh milk for breakfast from a milk seller. Like the girl in the picture on the right, she would take a jug to be filled. Although London was the biggest city in the world in the 19th century there were still farms on the out- skirts where cows were kept—in Chalk Farm, Hampstead and Camberwell. And even in the city you might hear a cow mooing near Fleet Street!

GETTING UP. Victorian bedrooms, like their other rooms, were crammed with pictures, ornaments and furniture. The four-poster beds were hung with thick curtains to keep out draughts. Some bedrooms might have coal fires, but most of them were chilly places—there was no central heating then, and no gas or electric fires. Notice the "day bed" or chaise longue behind the lady's maid in the picture opposite.

SERVANTS. The servants worked in the kitchens and rooms "below stairs" as you can see in the picture below. A narrow staircase led down here from the ground floor. It was shut off from the rest of the house by a swing door so that a butler or a maid could easily get by with a heavy tray. In 1850 about one-sixth of the population was "in service". Little girls began to work as servants when they were twelve.

BREAKFAST. The artist called the picture on the left "Domestic Bliss" because it shows a happy, contented family. The family would probably eat boiled eggs and toast, but they might have other things that are not so familiar to us—like muffins. The Victorians ate very large meals. Mrs. Beeton wrote a cookery book in 1861 which became famous. Her recipes certainly use a lot of food. In one recipe she says, "Take a dozen eggs and a pint of cream . . ."

THE NURSERY. In prosperous families the children were looked after by a nanny, or nurse, and their room was called the nursery. Nurse had to get the young children up and dressed in the mornings. On week days they had breakfast in the nursery. On Sunday mornings they joined Mama and Papa downstairs for family prayers and then breakfast. Boys wore dresses like little girls until they were about five and left the nursery.

FAMILY PRAYERS. In her book *Household Management* Mrs. Beeton said that morning prayers should be held at 8.45 a.m. and evening prayers at 10.00 p.m. And she meant every day! Certainly on Sundays family prayers took place in most Victorian homes. Servants attended as well. The father read from the Bible and said a prayer. He often gave a short talk in which he scolded or praised his children and servants if he thought they deserved it.

SUNDAY PAPERS. The gentleman reading his Sunday paper is not married. His manservant is looking after him. He may be reading the *Observer* or the *Sunday Times* which were respectable Sunday papers. More sensational Sunday papers were widely read by the working class. Papers like *Bell's Life in London* or *Reynold's News* were filled with stories of murder, child-kidnapping and other violent events.

PETTICOAT LANE. This Sunday morning market was held in the East End of London. In fact, you can still visit it today! Petticoat Lane attracted poorer people who went there to enjoy the bustle and the "patter" of salesmen, as well as the bargains. The market did a roaring trade in second-hand clothes. In Victorian times most people had to make their own clothes. Rich families took material to dressmakers who made up garments for them.

FETCHING SUNDAY DINNER. Bakers' shops often stayed open on Sundays and holidays, but not to bake bread. Poorer people brought their Sunday dinners to be cooked in the huge bakers' ovens. They could leave their pies or roasts with the baker, tell him how long they wanted them cooked, and go back later to collect a steaming hot dinner.

OFF TO CHURCH. It was a common sight in Victorian times to see the whole family walking to church, dressed in their best clothes. The children might feel very uncomfortable in thick stiff clothes, but they were not supposed to run or jump. Edmund Gosse, a famous writer, recalled that on Sundays he was not allowed to "enter the little chamber where I kept my treasures. I was hotly and tightly dressed all day as though ready at any moment to attend a funeral. . ."

FIRST AT CHURCH. Although they are very young the two children in the picture are dressed in their best clothes and are expected to behave just like adults in church. Many families had ten or more children; you can see why people said that "little children should be seen and not heard." But during the 19th century men and women began to understand that children were not just little adults. Some of the best children's books were written then— *Alice in Wonderland, The Water Babies,* and *The Secret Garden.*

Going to Church

The Victorians were very *pious*. Many of the great railway stations had Bibles on desks for the businessmen to read on their way to work. Church-going was an important Sunday duty. Far more people went regularly to church in those days than today. Going to church could also be a social event.

What were the churches like? The Church of England, or Anglican Church, was the "established" Church—it was the official church of the nation and government. The great cathedrals and most churches were Anglican. The Anglican Church thought that God had given each man a place in society:

> *The rich man in his castle;*
> *The poor man at his gate;*
> *God made them high or lowly*
> *And order'd their estate.*

In the new industrial towns like Manchester and Leeds which had sprung up around the mills and factories, most churches were *Non-conformist*. Non-conformists believed much the same as Anglicans, but their services were simpler. Methodists, Congregationalists and Baptists were all Non-conformists. Their clergymen preached thrift and hard work, so these churches appealed to the businessmen of the middle class.

The Victorians built more churches than any other people in English history. Many of them were built in the fashionable "Gothic" style. They looked like medieval buildings, with their spires, *pinnacles* and *gargoyles*.

THE ROYAL FAMILY. Queen Victoria, Prince Albert and their children always went to church on Sunday. They went to the Church of England when they were in London or Windsor, and to the Presbyterian, or Church of Scotland, when they were at their highland home in Balmoral. No amusements were allowed there on Sunday. The Queen's favourite Scottish servant, John Brown, is supposed to have found an artist near Balmoral Castle "scribblin and whustlin on the Sawbath." He handed the artist over to the police!

FAMILY PEWS. Look at the picture below. Even little children had to go to church every Sunday. In this family pew, mother and father can keep their eyes on all their children and stop any fighting. Well-to-do families who went to church a lot had their own pews specially reserved.

A PRIVATE PEW. Private pews had doors that could be locked from the inside. The people in these little rooms could quietly doze in the sermon without anyone noticing! In country churches the local squire usually owned a private pew. The one in the picture above belongs to the Duke of Wellington who won the battle of Waterloo in 1815.

A FASHIONABLE CONGREGATION. Fashionable ladies attended the Church of England, which was the Church of the nobility and gentry. "High Church" clergymen wore beautiful *vestments* and held elaborate services. They decorated their churches, and sometimes allowed candles and incense to be used. The Non-conformist services were "Low Church". There was no music or flowers, and the chapels had plain communion tables instead of high altars.

NON-CONFORMIST PREACHING. Look at the pictures above. Most Non-conformist churches were in the towns. They were red brick buildings called "chapels" and were plainly furnished inside. Non-conformist ceremonies were simpler than those of the Church of England. The sermon was the most important part of the service and Non-conformist ministers were known for their good sermons. In some cities these ministers went out into the streets to preach to people who did not go to church.

HER FIRST SERMON. This little girl is dressed in her best clothes to listen to her first sermon. Sermons were very long in Victorian churches, sometimes an hour. The clergyman took a text from the Bible and then told his congregation what they could learn from it. Some Victorian preachers were famous for their sermons. They were rather like actors, and could draw crowds to their churches to listen to them.

THE PEW OPENER. This little old lady on the left was employed to unfasten the doors of the pews. She probably laid out the hymn books and hassocks, too. She might be given an extra penny for her trouble by members of the congregation. She was one of the *lay* helpers or officials who worked for the Victorian churches. Organists, *vergers*, *sextons* and vestry clerks were also lay helpers.

TAKING THE COLLECTION. Collection money was used to keep the church in good repair or to buy new hymn books. Sometimes the clergyman had a special collection. This might be for a local charity, or for church missionary work abroad. In Victorian times many churches sent missionaries to foreign countries. You can see one in the picture below. The famous explorer, David Livingstone, took the message of the Bible to the natives of Central Africa.

GIVING ALMS. This ragged little boy in the picture above is begging a penny from a well-dressed lady. Middle-class Victorians thought it was their duty to give money to the poor. Notice how ragged he looks compared to the girl and the boy beside him. They are clean and neatly dressed and they have probably come from Sunday church. You can see the churchyard behind them and the boy is carrying a prayer book or a hymn book.

MEETING AFTER CHURCH. Victorian business-men often worked all day on Saturday. Sunday was one of the few times when they could meet their friends. Families usually lived near their church, so they could chat with friends as they walked home after the service. Some churches organized social events. The Congregationalist Church ran literary societies and tennis clubs.

SUNDAY SCHOOLS. Sunday schools helped to keep children out of mischief. Here they learned Bible stories, or they studied religious *tracts* specially written for children. There were no state schools in Victorian times. Sunday schools were often the only place where poor children could get an education. The Non-conformist churches had the most Sunday schools. By 1900 the Methodists had one million children at their schools.

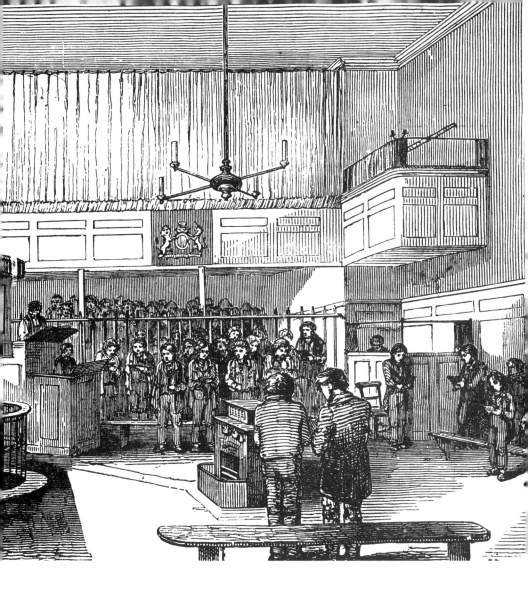

THE PRISON CHAPEL. This is the chapel of Newgate Prison. All prisoners had to attend services on Sunday. Elizabeth Fry, the Quaker prison reformer, visited Newgate to read the Bible to the prisoners. There were many Victorian men and women like her whose religious faith led them to do practical, social good.

Sunday in Town

Victorian families had many ways of spending a Sunday afternoon in town, even if the entertainment was rather quiet. After all, Sunday was a day of rest. Very strict Victorians thought that people should only go to church and read religious books on Sunday. People who did not believe in sitting at home all day could travel on horse buses and trams. But public transport was greatly reduced on Sundays. In 1879 a railway bridge over the River Tay collapsed, and many people lost their lives. Religious people thought this was God's punishment for running trains on Sunday.

As towns grew bigger, *municipal* councils were set up to take care of local affairs. The councils built parks and museums for townsfolk. These were very popular, especially on Sunday afternoons. In 1851 Queen Victoria's husband, Prince Albert, helped to organize a ''Great Exhibition of the industrial arts of all nations'' at the Crystal Palace in London. The Great Exhibition was very popular and visitors came from all over the country. It gave the Victorians a taste for exhibitions of all kinds, and they began to set up local museums. People who lived in the poorer parts of town spent their Sunday afternoon in a public house or watching the many street entertainers.

HORSE BUSES. Mr. Shillibeer's horse-drawn omnibuses first appeared on the London streets in 1829. They ran on Sundays and Londoners could travel on them to Richmond and Greenwich. But it cost $2\frac{1}{2}$p to ride in an omnibus which was quite a lot of money in those days. So poor people could not afford to use them. Omnibuses had an open-air top deck. In wet weather, there was a fight to sit inside!

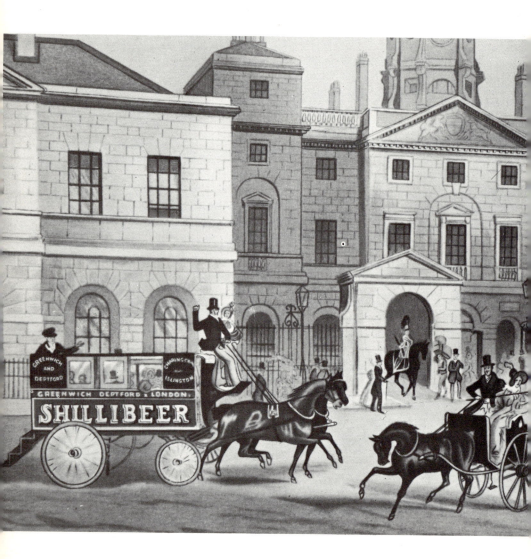

OMNIBUS CADS. The conductors of the first horse buses were known as "cads". They had all sorts of tricks for persuading passengers to board the bus when there were not really enough seats for them. They were fond of ringing the bell, too, before old ladies had time to get on board. Charles Dickens, the famous novelist, wrote a story about the first omnibus cad—a character called "Aggerawatin Bill".

CARRIAGE RIDES. The ladies and gentlemen who own these carriages are rich and comfortable. You can see their footmen on the outside seats. On a Sunday they could have a pleasant brisk drive through Hyde Park. But during the week Victorian London had traffic jams almost as bad as ours. As well as carriages, the streets were choked with carts, omnibuses and hansom cabs. There were no traffic lights, no police to direct traffic, and no rules about which side of the road to drive on!

PARKS. The Royal Parks in London, like Hyde Park and Regents Park, gave Londoners plenty of open spaces where they could enjoy themselves. And in the new industrial towns, municipal authorities were laying out parks for their citizens. The picture below shows one of these parks in Halifax. Notice the fountain and formal walks. This is a very sedate park designed for a gentle Sunday stroll. On the left you can see a mother holding her child by the hand.

CHILDREN'S GAMES. In the big London parks children could play all sorts of games. The wooded areas were ideal for hide-and-seek, and they could play cricket on the open spaces. The long gravel paths were perfect for bowling a hoop along. The little boy with the hoop must be quite young because he is still in skirts. He would be taken to the park by his nanny.

VAUXHALL GARDENS. Wealthier Victorians went to Vauxhall and Cremorne Gardens in London for entertainment. At night the gardens were ablaze with light. Fashionably-dressed men and women dined, danced and watched theatrical entertainers. On Sunday afternoons the gardens were a pleasant place for tea and a quiet stroll—no actors, jugglers or conjurors were allowed to perform then.

TEA GARDENS. These gardens with outdoor restaurants were not as elegant as Vauxhall, but their customers had plenty of fun. Most of the Londoners in the picture are clerks and shop assistants with their families. The children ate bread and butter, and the adults had tea or sometimes gin. The tea gardens were a favourite meeting place on Sunday afternoons for townspeople who had been busy in city offices all week.

CHURCH AGAIN. Quite often, Victorian families went to church in the morning, and again in the afternoon. The Victorians who went to church twice on Sundays were very strict about Sunday observance at home. They allowed no work to be done, so they had cold meat for dinner to avoid having to cook. When they were not at church, they read religious books. At Balmoral Queen Victoria insisted that guests go to their own rooms to sit in silence for most of the day.

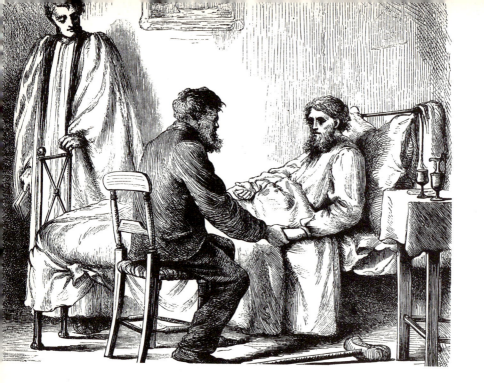

VISITING THE SICK. Look at the pictures above. It was the duty of Victorian clergymen to visit the sick in their parishes. Lay men and women undertook "good works" too, taking food or blankets to the poor and bedridden. Other visitors gave away religious tracts to the poor. But many poor people could not read, so these tracts were not very useful.

CHARITY OUTINGS. The picture opposite shows the children of Westminster ragged school on a Sunday outing. These schools were called "ragged" because they were set up by charitable Victorians to give free education to the poorest city children. They were taught to read, write and say the catechism. But many poor children could not go to these schools because their parents made them work as crossing sweepers or chimney sweeps to earn a few pennies.

ART GALLERIES. Victorian families often visited art galleries on Sunday afternoons. Many new galleries were built during Queen Victoria's reign. The picture on the left shows the art museum at Nottingham. There certainly are a lot of paintings crammed on the walls! The Victorians enjoyed paintings which were full of action. Queen Victoria's favourite artist was Sir Edward Landseer. He designed the four lions at the foot of Nelson's Column in Trafalgar Square.

EXHIBITIONS. Prince Albert helped to organize the Great Exhibition of 1851. It was a huge success, and over six million visitors came to see it. Prince Albert used the profit from the Exhibition to buy land in Kensington in London. The Natural History Museum, the Geological Museum and the Victoria and Albert Museum were built there. The Victorians liked to think they were learning something, as well as enjoying themselves, when they spent their Sundays at the museum.

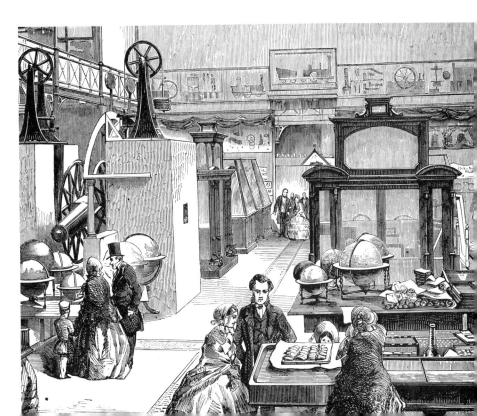

VISITING FRIENDS. There were strict rules of social *etiquette* in Victorian times. Ladies and gentlemen could not just drop in on their friends whenever they felt like it. Afternoon tea, however, was one of the times when people were expected to "call". If the friends were out, the visitors could leave their card with the maid to show that they had called. This had their name and address printed on it. Sometimes a visitor would write a message on it, as the lady on the left is doing.

POLITICAL MEETINGS. Political meetings were held in Trafalgar Square on Sundays as they often are now. The two main political parties in the Victorian Parliament were the Liberals and the Tories. Only men who owned a certain amount of property were allowed to vote. No women could vote. The Socialists tried to get votes for the poor. These pictures show a Socialist demonstration. It must have been a lively one, because the police are breaking up the scuffle which followed!

TEMPERANCE MEETINGS. The Victorians saw that heavy drinking caused a great deal of misery. Some fathers spent all their wages in the pub, and left their wives and children to starve. The *Temperance Movement* was started to make people give up "the demon drink". Huge meetings were held all over the country like the one in the picture above. Speakers urged their audience to give up beer and spirits, and drink tea instead.

PUBLIC HOUSES. In spite of the Temperance Movement, many poor people still drank gin. Gin was very cheap, and the poor drank it to make them forget their hard lives. The public houses, or "gin palaces", were gaily decorated and very warm so that people preferred to stay there rather than go back to their slum houses. The picture on the right shows the evils of a public house. The woman in the centre is giving gin to her baby!

51

BARREL ORGANS. Barrel organists were well-known street entertainers in Victorian times. Usually the barrel organist and his monkey stayed in the poorer parts of the city. Richer people would not be pleased to have their Sunday rest disturbed by his jangling music. You can see his monkey, dressed in a soldier's hat, sitting on the organ. The barefoot children dancing here have nowhere to play except the street.

DANCING BEARS. Dancing bears were quite a common street entertainment. The bear wore a muzzle and usually had his teeth drawn and his claws clipped. The bear's owner made him "dance" for money. He led him around the streets on a leash. The poor animal did not have a very happy life.

Sunday in the Country

Steam power was one of the greatest inventions of the 19th century. It drove the ships, the factory machines, and the railways that made Britain a great industrial country—the "workshop of the world." The first steamship crossed the Atlantic in 1838. By 1870 steam power was a cheap form of transport. Railways were driven by steam engines. Railway lines covered the whole country and linked all the large towns. Victorian families who wanted to get out of town on Sunday could take day trips, or excursions, on steam boats or trains.

Train excursions to the seaside were very popular. The Victorians liked to relax on the beach—although they took off very few clothes. A sun tan was not admired, and ladies carried *parasols* to protect their pale complexions.

The countryside was another favourite place to spend a Sunday afternoon. Townspeople did not have to travel far to reach it. London was much smaller than it is now, and there were fields and farms where today's suburbs stand. Church groups and Sunday schools arranged picnics in the country, and sports and games were played. The rules for games like tennis and football were made in the Victorian age. The bicycle was also invented at this time. It was a cheap form of transport and a healthy exercise at the same time.

STEAMER OUTINGS. The ladies and gentlemen in the picture on the left are about to board the steamers at the pier. A day trip on a steamer made a marvellous Sunday outing. The passengers played games on deck, or walked up and down enjoying the fresh air. Londoners went to Greenwich, or further afield to Gravesend or Margate; but the journey itself was the real treat. The travellers ate and drank a great deal, especially oysters, shrimps and beer. They had noisy sing-songs on the way home.

ON THE RIVER. This busy scene shows Sunday afternoon boating on the River Thames near Henley. The Victorian gentlemen are wearing quite different clothes from their usual dark suits and tall hats. Their boating clothes are loose and light coloured. One gentleman on the right is wearing a straw hat called a "boater". The ladies are wearing dresses gathered up at the back into *bustles*.

EXCURSION TRAINS. Thomas Cook organized the first railway excursion in 1841. He hired a train from the Midland Railway Company to take 570 passengers from Leicester to a temperance meeting at Loughborough. You can see the train setting off in the picture opposite. He did a great deal of business at the time of the Great Exhibition in 1851. He ran cheap day trips from all over the country to the Exhibition. Five years later he arranged the first railway tour of the whole country.

TRIPS TO BRIGHTON. "To Brighton and back for 3s. 6d." is the title of this painting. It shows the passengers on a cheap excursion, arranged by one of the railway companies. The carriage is open at the sides, which means it must be "third class". First and second class carriages were closed and had padded seats instead of wooden benches. There were no refreshment cars on these trains, but they made long stops at stations so that passengers could get out and buy food.

AT THE SEASIDE. The Victorians were really the
first people to enjoy the pleasures of the seaside.
For years people had gone to seaside resorts for their
health, but not for fun. The railways made travel much

cheaper than it had been by stage coach, so families began to go to the sea for holidays and outings. This picture shows the beach at Scarborough. You can see that the rich rode in their carriages along the sands.

BEACHWEAR. Children were sometimes allowed to take off their shoes and socks on the beach. But as you can see, they wore far more clothes than children today at the seaside. Gwen Raverat wrote a book about her own Victorian childhood. When playing in the garden, the children wore "thick, black woolly stockings and high boots. We always wore, too, very long, full overalls with long sleeves, and, of course, hats or caps of some sort."

THE PROMENADE. Most seaside towns built
promenades, or "proms", along their sea fronts.
Visitors walked up and down in their best clothes
enjoying the view of the sea and the fresh air. They
sang a song about it:

Oh, I do like to be beside the seaside,
Oh, I do like to be beside the sea.
Oh, I do like to stroll along the prom, prom, prom,
Where the brass bands play, tiddley om pom pom!

CHILDRENS' SERVICES. This unusual picture shows how the Victorians managed to bring religion into every activity—even outings to the seaside.

This is a special Sunday service for children on holiday in Hastings. The ladies are holding parasols to keep the sun off their faces.

COCKNEYS IN THE COUNTRY. Excursions to the country were almost as much fun as going to the seaside. This was especially true for poor city children who lived in cramped slum houses. The artist who drew the picture above hoped to make rich people understand that poor folk should be "permitted to enjoy themselves, now and then, in the fields and woods."

CRINOLINES. This drawing makes a joke about the size of a lady's *crinoline*. These huge skirts were held up by a cage of cane or metal. They were very fashionable. Victorian ladies wore these skirts on their Sunday outings in the country. It must have been hard to get through the farmers' gates. Even the cow seems to be staring at the strange sight!

PICNICS. Picnics combined two of the Victorians' greatest pleasures: the open air and plenty of food. Not everyone here is enjoying himself. Some picnickers are very alarmed by the two little frogs! Victorian picnics were formal affairs, arranged well in advance. The picknickers went prepared—their hampers were filled with plenty of food and drink, glasses, plates, table-cloths, and knives and forks.

COUNTRYFOLK. Rural England in Queen Victoria's time was cut off from the bustling life of the towns. Businessmen travelled in trains across the countryside from one big city to another. The old roads between the villages and country towns were hardly used. This country family is enjoying a peaceful Sunday dinner outside their thatched cottage.

VILLAGE CRICKET MATCHES. Sometimes church clubs organized cricket matches or other sporting events. This picture shows a village cricket match held on a Sunday afternoon. Everyone from the local squire to the farm hands took part. Their wives looked after the refreshments. The farm labourers are wearing their traditional smocks. One old man is sharing a bottle of beer with a rather stiff Victorian gentleman in a top hat.

COUNTRY PUBS. The ale-house and church were the two social centres of every English village. The picture opposite shows two farm workers having a pint of beer at their local pub. Sunday was their only day off. They had to work very hard, and their wages were low. Many of them went away to work in the mills and factories of Manchester or Birmingham. But life was healthier for countryfolk: at least they had fresh air and home-grown food.

ARCHERY. The ladies and gentlemen in the picture above are taking part in an archery contest on a pleasant Sunday afternoon in the country. Archery was very well suited to Victorian ladies. Since they did not have to run about, they were not bothered by their long full skirts. They wore special "archery dresses" of Lincoln green with matching feather hats.

LAWN TENNIS. The very first lawn tennis champion-
ship took place at Wimbledon in 1877. Many
churches, like the Congregationalists, had their own
tennis clubs. The rackets used then were smaller
than ours, and they were pear-shaped. Gentlemen
played in long white flannel trousers. The ladies'
games must have been very boring—they could not
run about much because of their long skirts. They
had to pat the ball gently to and fro. They wore hats,
too!

CYCLING. Many people bought bicycles in Victorian times. Early models were called "boneshakers". Their solid rubber wheels gave a very bumpy ride. Cycling in the parks and in the countryside was a pleasant way to spend a Sunday afternoon. Ladies enjoyed bicycling, but it was years before they wore suitable clothes. In America, the famous Mrs. Bloomer wore baggy trousers for cycling. They were jokingly called "bloomers".

PUNCH AND JUDY. The Punch and Judy man went about the countryside with his theatre and his puppets packed up on his back. He stopped wherever he could get an audience and set up his show. He often played on the beach. The picture on the right shows him at a country fête. The story of Punch and Judy's adventures never changed, but it was always a treat for the Victorians who had to make their own entertainment.

Home Sweet Home

Theatres and *music halls* were not allowed to open on Sundays in Victorian England, and of course there was no cinema or television. Although the main streets in big towns were lit by gas lights, the smaller streets were dark. People usually stayed at home and entertained themselves in the evenings. Most Victorian families were large. Queen Victoria herself had nine children, and families of twenty were not unusual. So Victorian children had plenty of brothers and sisters to play with. It was easy for them to arrange homemade entertainments.

If you think of the Victorian house in the first chapter, you will remember how little heating it had. After tea the whole family gathered in the dining room where a fire was lit. They spent the evening reading, knitting or embroidering, playing games or making music. Sometimes the family sat together round a table to read or work by the light of an oil or gas lamp. Gas lighting was invented in the 19th century. The Victorians thought that "Satan finds mischief for idle hands;" they liked to fill their leisure hours with activity.

TEA TIME. This old photograph shows a Victorian family at tea time. The room has elaborate furnishings. Notice the patterned tablecloth, the carving on the chair, and the gilt mirror with its candle holders. The ladies are wearing crinolines, and the older one a bonnet as well. Everyone has a solemn Sunday face. Ladies were told to say "prunes and prisms" before entering a room, so that their faces would look prim. Try saying it yourself!

WRITING LETTERS. The maids in the picture below are probably writing to their sweethearts. There was a Sunday postal delivery in Victorian times so they could expect to receive a letter, too. The Penny Post was started by a man called Roland Hill in 1840. A letter could be sent anywhere in England for a penny as long as it was only one sheet of paper. The Victorians wrote all over the sheet to get all their news on it. They wrote another letter on top of the first one but with the lines running from top to bottom instead of side to side. This made it rather difficult to read!

GAS LIGHTING. Gas lighting was used in the main streets of the West End of London as early as 1819. But the Victorians were slow to use it in their homes. At first it was dangerous and likely to explode! A maid servant who was used to blowing out candles would try to blow out a gas jet—forgetting to turn off the gas—with disastrous results. By 1900 however, many homes had gas and electricity.

READING ALOUD. Reading aloud was a favourite pastime in the Victorian age. On Sunday father might read from the Bible, a book of sermons, or even a popular novel if the family was not too strict. In Queen Victoria's time many new printing machines were invented, and books became quite cheap to buy. Also, more people went to school and learned to read. There was a great demand for books of all kinds.

THE SUNDAY AT HOME

A Family Magazine for Sabbath Reading.

INSIDE A CAFFRE KRAAL.

THE FOUNTAIN KLOOF:

OR, MISSIONARY LIFE IN SOUTH AFRICA.

CHAPTER VII.—A MIDSUMMER CHRISTMAS.

It dawned with a brilliance such as we northerns have never beheld, and five hours earlier than the pallid December light would kindle in our cold English east on the contemporary day. A bright rose colour was painted along the verge of the clear vault, and gradually diffused upward, like tides of a glorious sea gaining flow over a star-strand. The strange table-tops of the mountains were gilded with a ruddy glow, warming the naked crags as a smile warms the hardest fac[e] before, from the lowlands, the cause of all the glo[ry] was visible, rolling upwards a pure golden ball ov[er] purple hills to the eastward.

News had not yet come. The messengers had r[e-]ceived orders to retrace their steps rapidly on t[he] earliest discovery of the savage army said to be on i[ts] march: Mr. Enfield knew that he could rely on the[m.] He was confident now that the reports had been gross[ly] exaggerated, and the warlike movement, if such existe[d] at all, was limited to tribe against tribe.

His rhetoric did not very much convince the mi[....]

SUNDAY READING. This magazine is what strict Victorian fathers read to their children on Sundays. It contains one episode of a serial story about an African missionary. Many books were published as serials during Victorian times. The novels of famous writers like Charles Dickens and William Makepeace Thackeray were published in monthly parts. Each part cost a shilling (5p). The authors sold thousands of copies of their books because everyone could afford to buy them this way.

SKETCHING. The family in the picture below is spending the evening looking at father's portfolio of pictures. Victorian tourists liked to paint water colours while they were on holiday. They carried brushes, a paint box, and a folding easel in a knapsack. They brought back their water colours as souvenirs, just as we take snapshots today. Young ladies were taught to sketch portraits and scenery as part of their education.

SEWING. This was one of the few "jobs" that a Victorian lady was allowed to do. The Victorians were very fond of little ornaments of all kinds. Ladies embroidered *antimacassars*. They put them over the backs of chairs to protect them from gentlemen's hair oil. Or they made pin-cushions, pen-wipers for cleaning quill pens, and even frilly pantalettes to cover the naked legs of pianos and tables! Of course women sewed practical things, too. They made most of their clothes at home.

MUSICAL EVENINGS. Musical entertainments at home gave Victorian girls a chance to show off their talents. The young lady at the piano has a gentleman to turn over the pages of her music. Sentimental ballads were very popular, like "Home, Sweet Home" or "My Luv is like a Red, Red Rose." When a Victorian family held a musical evening they asked their friends to bring their own music and instruments. After the solo performances the whole party sang and played together.

MAGIC LANTERN SHOWS. Look at the picture above. Victorian children enjoyed the "magic lantern" just as we enjoy the cinema and television today. It was a simple projector which could shine a picture of a drawing or photograph onto a white screen. There was no sound or movement, of course, but Victorian children saw all kinds of shows—pictures of wild animals and foreign lands, or fairy tales and exciting adventures.

PRINTING AT HOME. Here is a very busy family. The machine on the table is a small printing press. The girl on the right is choosing pieces of type for her brother to set up in the press. The parents are reading some of the results of their children's work. This is a good example of how the Victorians used their leisure to do useful things that were fun too.

INDOOR GAMES. Some families did not believe in playing games on Sundays. Many people thought cards were "wicked". But in some large households everyone might take part in innocent fun like guessing games or consequences. They might even play hide and seek or hunt the thimble. The people in the picture above are playing a game called "Snap-dragon".

EVENING HYMNS. Sunday ended, as it began, with family prayers. The Victorians thought all families should look like the happy group in this picture. The room is comfortably furnished with heavy draperies and solid furniture. The two older children are singing the evening hymn to the rest of the family.

AND SO TO BED. This Victorian child is saying her evening prayers to her mother before going to sleep. Many religious books, hymns and prayers were written specially for children in the Victorian age. Here is a child's prayer:

Gentle Jesus, meek and mild,
Look upon a little child.
Pity my simplicity,
Suffer me to come to thee.

Table of Dates

1837	Queen Victoria comes to the throne
1840	Rowland Hill starts the penny post. A letter could be sent anywhere in England for one penny
1842	Mines Act stops women and young children working in coal mines
1846	Repeal of the Corn Laws. Cheap foreign corn is allowed into England so poor people can afford to buy bread
1847	Ten Hours Act stops factory workers working more than ten hours a day
1851	Great Exhibition is held at the Crystal Palace in London
1859	Charles Darwin publishes *The Origin of Species* which showed that men were descended from monkey-like creatures
1867	Second Reform Act gives the vote to skilled workers as well as the middle classes
1870	Education Act provides free elementary schools for all children
1897	Queen Victoria's Diamond Jubilee—she had ruled for sixty years
1901	Death of Queen Victoria. Her son comes to the throne as Edward VII

New Words

Antimacassar	An embroidered cloth laid over the back of a chair to protect it from gentlemen's hair oil—which was made from macassar oil
Bustle	Padding in a woman's skirt to puff it out in the back
Crinoline	A wide circular skirt held up by steel hoops
Etiquette	The rules of polite behaviour
Gargoyles	Fantastic carvings of men and beasts used to decorate Gothic buildings
Laymen	People who are not clergymen or in religious orders
Municipal	Local government
Music hall	Place of entertainment where the Victorians could enjoy singing and dancing
Non-conformist	Someone who does not agree with the Church of England
Parasol	Small umbrella carried by ladies to protect their faces from the sun
Pinnacles	Little pointed towers which decorated the roofs of Gothic buildings
Pious	Very religious

Respectable	Honest and upright
Scullery	Small room off the kitchen with a sink where the washing up was done
Sexton	The official in charge of the upkeep of a church and the churchyard
Temperance Movement	A group of people who tried to make other Victorians give up all alcoholic drinks
Tracts	Short printed leaflets about religion
Verger	A church official who shows people to their seats
Vestments	The clergyman's official clothes
Victorian	The name given to the years when Queen Victoria ruled Great Britain, 1837–1901, and to the people who lived at that time

More Books

Brown, Ivor. *Dickens and his World* (Lutterworth Press, 1970). A clear and well-illustrated account of the life of the famous novelist.

Dickens, Charles. *David Copperfield* (Penguin, 1966). The adventures of one Victorian boy who escaped from a wicked stepfather to become a famous writer.

Quennell, M. & C. H. B. *A History of Everyday Things in England,* III, IV (Batsford, 1958). A history with pictures of all the things the Victorians used in their everyday lives.

Reader, W. J. *Life in Victorian England* (Batsford, 1964). A good general picture for older readers of the social life of the time.

Rooke, Patrick, *The Age of Dickens* (Wayland, 1970). Victorian England in the words of people living at the time.

Hart, Roger. *English Life in the Nineteenth Century* (Wayland, 1971). A vivid account of social life, with more than a hundred pictures, many in colour

Index

Picture Credits